LONG STORY SHORT

D1520428

LONG STORY SHORT

*Dwelling in the Good News
of the Great Story*

Dillon T. Thornton

WIPF & STOCK · Eugene, Oregon

To my Theology on Tap group:
Good dudes
who together endeavor to dwell
in the good news of the Great Story.

CONTENTS

SCRIPTURE AS STORY

"I love you 3000."

—*TONY STARK*

AS A FATHER, THERE are certain things I want to teach my children: spiritual disciplines, like Bible study and prayer; the basics of fitness and nutrition; the importance of reading and being a lifelong learner; and of course, the subtle art of a well-placed movie line. In my house, we quote movie lines. It's an unending game. At any moment, with no notice at all, someone will quote a line from one of our favorite movies, and the other members of the family will rush to guess the reference. My wife, Jamie, will say, "Muscle up, buttercup!" and someone will shout *"Moana!"* I'll say, "Snakes, why did it have to be snakes?" and someone will shout, *"Raiders of the Lost Ark!"* One of my sons will jump into the pool and let out a midair cry of "For Asgard!" and we'll all say *"Thor: Ragnarok!"*

We're able to recognize these quotes, because we know the movies so well. We've seen them dozens and dozens of times. In each case, the quote reminds us of the overall story of the movie; and the story of the movie gives deeper meaning to the quote. A great example of this point is found in one of our all-time favorite films, *Avengers: Endgame*. (Resolute readers who endure to the end of this book will learn of my obsession with all things Marvel.) When Tony Stark's daughter says, "I love you 3000," we who know the whole story understand why this simple line is so meaningful. Because in the end, Tony will give his life to save his daughter, his family, and humanity, and he will repeat this line to his little girl. They serve as his last words. Those who know only the beginning of *Endgame* will hear in "I love you 3000" the cuteness of a kindergartner. But those who know the whole story will hear in these same words the ultimate sacrifice of the story's hero. Knowledge of the whole gives deeper meaning to the individual parts.

My years of ministry experience are now of drinking age. Over the past two decades, I've talked with thousands of Christians: from Dunedin, New Zealand, to Dunedin, Florida. And among the various traditions and denominations, I've discovered a common denominator. Most Christians I've met can cite or at least paraphrase certain verses from the Bible: John 3:16; Rom 3:23; Phil 4:13 (usually out of context). But relatively few seem to understand how these individual lines fit into the larger story of the Bible. Not long ago, I had a conversation with a friend—we'll call him Captain Kirk—who admitted that, though he's been around Bible teaching for much of his life, he only recently discovered that the Bible is in fact one big story. "For the longest time," he said, "I thought it was more like a set of encyclopedias or a mini library of loosely connected writings."

Captain Kirk isn't alone. Many readers think of the Bible as a confused mixture of entries, episodes, characters, and commands. Sixty-six books, written by some thirty authors, scattered over a period of roughly fifteen hundred years, including virtually every genre known to man. Clearly, the Bible consists of many parts. Yet, it communicates a meta-narrative, one great story, the drama of redemption. And when we understand this story and find our place within it, it brings us unparalleled purpose and hope.

In the chapters that follow, I will tell the story of Scripture, from Genesis to Revelation. Unlike other Old Testament or New Testament surveys, this book is not intended for seminary students or pastors. It avoids the dense footnotes and scholarly nomenclature common to this category. I hope it will read more like a story and less like a textbook. In order to make the long story *short*, I've exercised the discipline of selectivity. Of course, much more could have been said on the subjects of creation, rebellion, promise, and so on. And much more has been said elsewhere (see the bibliography at the end of the book[1]). But again, this book is not intended for highly motivated ministry practitioners but for crazy-busy parents and plumbers; for elementary teachers and engineers; for software developers and construction workers. This book is for the ordinary, everyday follower of Jesus with a sincere love for his or her Lord but with no specialization in biblical languages, customs, or history. If you have no idea what year the Northern Kingdom of Israel fell, and if you couldn't locate ancient Assyria on a map if your life depended on it, then this book is for you. If you're the guy who never read the book in high school, always opting for the CliffsNotes, then, as Doc Holliday says in the movie *Tombstone*, "I'm your huckleberry." In fact, I've written this book with the hopes that it might be the first book about the Bible you've ever read, and that, in reading it, the Spirit will awaken you to God's gracious and persistent plan for the world and your place within his plan. Christians, as we will discover together, are not just *storytellers*; we are *story dwellers*. And this marvelous truth changes everything.

1. My own thinking and writing (including the present volume) have been shaped significantly by Bartholomew and Goheen, *The Drama of Scripture*; Beale and Kim, *God Dwells Among Us*; Dever, *The Message of the Old Testament* and *The Message of the New Testament*; Goldsworthy, *According to Plan* and *The Goldsworthy Trilogy*; Hunter and Wellum, *Christ from Beginning to End*. I owe an enormous debt of gratitude to these authors especially.

1

CREATION

The story of Scripture begins with the people of God living in the good place God designed for them to fulfill their unique purpose.

The God of Creation

THE OPENING SCENE OF any story is worth watching carefully. The first moments of *The Dark Knight* set the sinister tone for the movie. *The Lion King* begins with an effervescent celebration of new life. The beginning of *Spectre* assures the viewer: Bond's still got it.

The opening scene of the biblical story introduces the God with whom everything begins. The God of the Bible is revealed to us as a triunity, a fellowship of Father, Son, and Holy Spirit. According to Gen 1:1–2, the Father and the Holy Spirit were present and active in the very beginning. In John 1:1, we find an echo of the Genesis account: "In the beginning was the Word, and the Word was with God, and the Word was God . . . . All things were made through him." John makes it clear that "the Word" is a reference to the Son, Jesus Christ. So the story of the Bible, and the story of the world, begins with the Father, the Son, and the Holy Spirit. The triune reality of the biblical God is a mystery; Christians affirm this truth without fully understanding it. But our lack of complete comprehension doesn't bother us. A God small enough to be fully understood wouldn't be large enough to be worshiped. Perhaps at times you've thought that the Father was the main character of the Old Testament, the Son the main character of the Gospels, and the Spirit the main character of Acts and everything that follows. Or perhaps you've thought that the Son began in Bethlehem and the Spirit began on the day of Pentecost (Acts 2). On the contrary, Gen 1 and John 1 combine to show us the *eternal* God, the *triune* Creator, the Maker of all things.

The belief that God is the Maker of all things is the premise for the belief that he is sovereign, or powerful, over all things. If I give my friend Todd a pile of wood, he can build just about anything. If I give my wife Jamie a canvas and a supply of paint, she can create a beautiful piece of art. They get these capacities from their Creator, and you and I have our own creative gifts. But there's an important difference between the way we create and the way God created: God created from nothing. In the very beginning, there was no material, no wood, no paint. There was only God himself. And from the nothing, God made something. Why did God choose to create? It wasn't because he was lonely. Among the members of the Trinity, there has been perfect communion and completion for all eternity. Therefore, we can't say that God created the world because he was somehow unfulfilled. Nor can we say that God created because he needed us or any part of creation. "Need" is a creaturely word. Creation, then, is not an act of necessity but of charity. God *loved* his creation into existence. He loved us into existence.

The Community of Creation

By causing the creation to come into existence, God established it as his own vast kingdom, the theater where his plan will be played out. God brought into existence a creation that is characterized by beauty, order, and purpose. Light and darkness; sky, sea, and land; sun, moon, and stars; plants and trees; all the living creatures.

Think of the beauty of it all. Think of the complexity of ecosystems, plants, animals, and other organisms, as well as weather and landscapes, all working together to nourish life. God is the Designer of all of this. Creation is not only about beginnings—it is also about order; about how God, by his intricate design, sustains life. This beautiful community of creation is composed of countless creatures, and each one has a unique purpose in God's plan. My wife insists that cockroaches are the exception to this; these spine-chilling pests are of the devil, she says. Admittedly, you and I might not know why some creatures exist. But whether our finite minds understand their purpose, all creatures matter, because all originate with God.

A related subject that warrants at least a few minutes of our time is the relationship between faith and science. Certain people claim that Genesis affirms one thing about the origins of the world while science affirms something altogether different. "Therefore," they say, "we must accept one and reject the other." Faith and science are pitted against each other, as if they're tributes from separate districts in *The Hunger Games*, and only one may live. In actuality, faith and science are much more like Katniss and Peeta; they're friends, not foes. Good science and good theology are quite compatible. Genesis clearly affirms that the vast world in which we live and the complex community of creation was established by the action of God. But Genesis is not interested in telling us *how* God created. Precisely how long it took God to create the world and the means he chose to achieve his purpose are questions Genesis does not answer. The word our English Bibles translate as "day" can refer to periods of time longer than twenty-four hours. Some Christians choose to believe the world was created in six twenty-four-hour days, and they further conclude, based on the genealogies of the Old Testament, that the earth is between six and ten thousand years old. Other possibilities include the view that "day" in Gen 1 refers to much longer periods of time and the view that "day" is not intended to tell us anything about time; rather, it is a literary device used by the author in order to communicate the story of creation in terms we can understand. These interpretations of Genesis leave ample room for the conclusion of scientists, based on the fossil record, that life is billions (not thousands) of years old. The bottom line is this: whatever the mechanisms or time period, God is responsible for the community of creation and our purposeful place within it.

In Gen 1:26, we're told that God created humanity in his image. It's the image of God that sets humanity apart, that distinguishes us from the rest of creation. This incredibly important concept in the story of Scripture means at least three things. First and foremost, it means that we are designed to live in a unique type of relationship with God, our Creator; we are made for intimate, personal fellowship with him. Nothing will satisfy us but God. As the fourth-century philosopher Augustine put it in his *Confessions*, "our heart is restless until it rests in you [God]." Second, we are designed to live in relationships with others that reflect and showcase God's love. And third, we are designed to reflect God's loving rule as we exercise dominion over his creation. In the ancient world, a king would create an image to remind everyone of his role as the ruler of the land. The intent of the image was to draw the people to the king. According to Gen 1, you and I are the image intended to draw people to the King of all kings, the sovereign Ruler of all. We were created to showcase the loving and caring rule of God. We are underkings, vice-regents, royal stewards. We have a specific role to play within this vast kingdom God has created.

The Goal of Creation

One of the things that is clear in Genesis is that God's creation is not static. Creation is *going somewhere*, and we have an important role to play in this journey. Genesis 1:27–28 is commonly referred to as the cultural mandate. This short but stout passage reveals both our identity and our responsibility, or purpose. The most important thing to be said about our identity is that we are created in the image of God, which we've already discussed. The passage also affirms that God created us male and female. Gender and sexuality are part of God's design for his good creation. God wired us for intimacy; he engineered the male and the female for an erotic and procreative union. Our God-given responsibility, or purpose, cannot be fully fulfilled if we reject his design for gender and sexuality. What is our God-given responsibility? "Be fruitful and multiply, fill the earth and subdue it, and have dominion" (Gen 1:28). God says to the man and the woman, "Have lots of sex and rule the world." Whoever said Christianity was no fun? The cultural mandate is a call to populate the earth with image bearers, to fill the world with people who live in fellowship with God, who reflect his love, and who care for his creation. The terms "subdue" and "dominion" introduce the idea of development or cultivation. Genesis 1 not only teaches us that every *person* is significant but also that every *vocation* that contributes to the flourishing of creation is a holy calling. The cultural mandate challenges us to undertake the study of God's world and to come to know this world as well as we can so that we might appropriately rule in it and serve our Creator well. In this light, science, art, and other forms of work we tend to label "secular" ought instead to be viewed as high and holy callings. Do you see how the story of Scripture already is beginning to re-story your life? Your identity, your relationships, and even your vocation all take on a far deeper meaning when viewed within the context of the story of Scripture.

2

REBELLION

A major feature of any story is the conflict, the problem that arises and that only the hero of the story can solve. In the biblical story, the conflict is a cosmic one; the problem affects all of God's good creation.

The Beauty and Activity of Eden

IN THE BEGINNING, GOD loved his good creation into existence, and he gave humanity everything: intimate fellowship with their Creator, peaceful relationships within the community of creation, and purposeful existence in the beautiful place God created for them. But in Gen 3, a calamity occurs, simply and ominously referred to as the fall of mankind. The man and the woman, Adam and Eve, were tempted, they succumbed to the temptation, and the results were tragic. The events of Gen 3 radically altered human nature and the course of history.

We need to return to the initial setting of the story. When God created the world, he called humanity to an elevated position within the created order, and he crafted a special place for us to carry out our purpose: the garden of Eden. Though Eden is referred to as a garden, it is pictured as a sanctuary or temple.

In Eden, God is present with his image bearers; they have fellowship with him, serve him, and worship him. When God says to the man and woman, "Be fruitful and multiply and fill the earth and subdue it" (Gen 1:28), he gives them the mission of extending the beauty and activity of Eden to the ends of the earth. The call is to populate the world with worshipers. The Great Commission, given in the New Testament (Matt 28:18–20), grows out of this mandate in Genesis. Throughout the biblical story, the mission is the same: multiply image bearers; populate the world with worshipers; make disciples of all nations; expand the beauty and activity of Eden until it fills the entire earth. A crucial detail is that this mission is given within the context of a relationship, and it cannot be fully fulfilled if the relationship is lost. We are image bearers created to reflect God's love, but we cannot reflect God if we do not have fellowship with him. We can't showcase God's love if we don't know God himself.

When God created the garden-temple of Eden, he gave Adam every tree for food, except one: the tree of the knowledge of good and evil. Only two of the trees in Eden are mentioned by name: the tree of life and the tree of the knowledge of good and evil. This story is the only place in Scripture where this mysterious tree of knowledge is mentioned. We might think that this tree looked dark or forbidding—like the Whomping Willow in *Harry Potter and the Prisoner of Azkaban*—but there was nothing inherently repulsive about it, because it was part of God's good and beautiful creation. We might also misinterpret the name of the tree, asking, "Why would God withhold knowledge from humanity?" But this is to miss the point of the tree entirely. God *did* desire for the man and woman to have knowledge, knowledge that he himself would communicate within the context of the loving relationship he had established with them. God was to be the source of knowledge, the source of all truth. The tree of knowledge provided a test of loyalty: Will Adam and Eve depend on their Creator for their understanding of the world and their place within it? Or will they seek to become autonomous, self-ruling, self-serving?

The Tempter and Temptation

When the curtains rise and part 2 of the story begins, we meet a new character: a seductive serpent. We are not told where the talking serpent comes from or who he is. It is not until the very end of the biblical story that we discover his true identity. Revelation 12:9 refers to "that ancient serpent, who is called the devil and Satan, the deceiver of the whole world." Where did Satan come from? And how did he become so evil? The Bible doesn't give us a definitive answer to these questions. And how exactly does Satan work through the serpent? Yet another mystery. In Scripture, we catch only occasional glimpses of this shadowy adversary. But this shouldn't surprise us. The Bible exists to give us a deeper understanding of God. It is not designed to arm us with encyclopedic knowledge of the enemy but only that which is necessary for comprehending the world in which we live. What is clear from Gen 3 is that the serpent is opposed to God's good purpose for Adam and Eve. His own "glorious purpose," to use Loki's expression, is to lead humanity away from God.

Temptation is the serpent's specialty from the beginning. In the Genesis narrative, he targets the woman, probably because he thought the woman would be the easier of the two to deceive. Not because women are less intelligent or less resourceful than men. But because the woman had not received instruction directly from God. The command "You may surely eat of every tree of the garden except for the tree of knowledge" was given to the man in Gen 2:16–17. The woman is created in the following scene of Gen 2. So if chapter 2 is intended to be read chronologically, then Eve was not yet on the earth when God issued the prohibition. It would have been Adam's responsibility to pass on the Lord's instruction to his wife. And as we will see, either Adam failed as the family shepherd or Eve did not listen to her husband, because when she cites God's word, she does so incorrectly.

At first, the serpent's tactic is to create doubt: "Did God really say . . . ? Are you sure, Eve? Were you there? Did you hear it?" (see Gen 3:1). This prompts Eve to quote the Lord's command, but she modifies God's word in three ways. First, she minimizes God's provision. Eve says, "We may eat of the fruit of the trees in the garden" (Gen 3:2). God actually said, "You may *surely* or *freely* eat" (see Gen 2:16), indicating the abundance of his provision for the man and woman. Second, she adds to the prohibition. Eve says, "You shall not eat of the . . . tree . . . , neither shall you touch it" (Gen 3:3). But God said nothing about touching the tree. And third, she weakens the penalty. Eve says, "lest you die," indicating possibility (Gen 3:3). But God said, "In the day that you eat of it you shall *surely die*" (Gen 2:17, italics added).

Maybe Adam's instruction was imprecise, or maybe Eve did not listen attentively when her husband sought to pass on the instruction. Whatever happened, it's evident that Eve did not have an exact understanding of God's word. If she had, would she have been better prepared for what happens next? The serpent takes things further: from questioning God's word to attacking God's character. He now wants the woman to disregard the divine instruction altogether, to reject God outright. The serpent declares that the tree of knowledge will not lead to death. He pictures God as a liar and the tree as the path to true life, the key that will unlock everything God has been withholding from them. "In the garden, you have a good life, but you could have something far better!" the serpent says. Eve is deceived. Forgetting all that God had provided, she eats the fruit of the forbidden tree, and she shares the fruit with Adam. The family fails the test of loyalty. Will Adam and Eve depend on their Creator for their understanding of the world and their place within it? Or will they seek to become autonomous, self-ruling, self-serving? In eating the forbidden fruit, they answer emphatically, "We will go our own way. We will be our own gods." In lusting after a throne that was not theirs, they lost the privileges they already possessed.

The Tragic Results and First Gospel

Immediately, Adam and Eve experience shame, guilt, and fear. They hide from each other and from God. God approaches Adam, asking, "Have you eaten of the tree of knowledge?" Of course, God possesses all knowledge; he knows precisely what has transpired. His question provides Adam with an opportunity for confession. But Adam doesn't take responsibility for his actions. Instead, he blames the woman, and ultimately, he blames God: "The woman whom you gave to be with me, she gave me fruit of the tree, and I ate" (Gen 3:12). The woman in turn blames the serpent: "The serpent deceived me, and I ate" (Gen 3:13). Because God is the just King of creation, this rebellion against him, his abundant provision, and his good plan brings judgment.

The judgment on the woman introduces pain as part of the fallen world and conflict as a new reality of human relationships. The judgment on the man introduces conflict between humanity and creation itself. The man receives a dose of his own medicine. God was to exercise loving dominion over the man, but the man rebelled. Man was to exercise loving dominion over God's good creation, but now creation will rebel. Finally, there is the sentence of death. Death in Gen 2–3 must be understood in two ways. First, it refers to physical death. While we can presume that death existed in the plant and animal world prior to Gen 3 (because the man and woman were given plants to eat and because God created predatory animals), death becomes an inevitable reality for humanity as a result of our rebellion. In Gen 4, we read of the first murder. In Gen 5, we find a long list of genealogies, and the story usually ends with the same somber comment: "and he died." But there must be a second way of understanding death, because in Gen 2, God warned Adam, "*In the day* that you eat of it [the fruit] you shall surely die" (Gen 2:17, italics added). Adam dies physically, but not on this day. What, then, did God mean? The warning in Gen 2 refers to *spiritual death*. Simply stated, death is separation. Physical death is separation from the land of the living. Spiritual death is separation from God. And this is precisely what occurs on the day of rebellion. At the end of Gen 3, Adam and Eve are banished from the garden-temple of Eden, separated from the presence of God. And separated from God, they cannot possibly reflect God's love; they cannot fully fulfill their purpose on this planet.

These statements of judgment are declarations of how life must now be. The fall of Gen 3 is the explanation for all the brokenness in the world today. Why is there so much pain and suffering? Why is there conflict between individuals and countries? Why are there hurricanes and viruses? Why does death eventually come for us all? Why are all people sinners, separated from God and thus unable to fulfill our God-given purpose? All the defectiveness can be traced back to the rebellion in the garden-temple of Eden. From our first parents, we inherit a creation now full of brokenness and a condition of sinfulness. Adam and Eve's status when they exited Eden is our status as we enter this earth—separation.

But in the midst of the judgment, there is a message of grace. Where in the biblical story do we first find the good news of the gospel? Matthew? One of the prophets, perhaps? No, long before this. As soon as sin enters the world of mankind, the hope of the gospel is announced. According to Gen 3:15, the woman's offspring will one day defeat the serpent. Though the victory will come at a great cost.

3

PROMISE

The remainder of the Old Testament tells the story of how the Creator God called a people to be his partner in rescuing humanity and restoring all of creation.

Covenant: God Establishes His Promise

THE FALL OF MANKIND recorded in Gen 3 doesn't alter Adam and Eve's humanity or purpose. They remain in the image of God, though now their God-given purpose cannot be fully fulfilled because their fellowship with God has been broken. So, too, has their relationship with each other and with nature. Throughout the book of Genesis, the brokenness of the world manifests itself in many ways, including the first murder in chapter 4. In Gen 6, things reach such a low point that God sends a great flood, but he forms a covenant with Noah, promising that, despite the depths of humanity's evil, he will never again destroy the earth by flood. From Genesis forward, God enters into one formal relationship after another with chosen individuals as he works toward fulfilling the promise of Gen 3:15—the first gospel. The mandate first given to Adam and Eve is repeated to Noah: "Be fruitful and multiply and fill the earth" (Gen 9:1). Noah's family populates and cultivates, but sin continues to corrupt relationships and even cultural developments. In Gen 10, the nations that emerge from the descendants of Noah cooperate to construct an enormous tower. The Tower of Babel is a work of unified pride. It's a repetition of the rebellion in Eden, another attempt to become autonomous, self-ruling, and self-serving, though now the rebellion occurs on a grand social scale. God judges the people's arrogance by confusing their language and scattering them across the earth.

In Gen 12, God directs his gracious gaze to a man named Abraham. Abraham and his descendants are the major focus of the remainder of Genesis. As he did with Noah, God establishes a covenant with Abraham. The covenants are like the backbone of the biblical story, structuring the meta-narrative. Theologians and biblical scholars commonly define a covenant as a bond in blood, sovereignly administered. This requires some unpacking. As a *bond*, a covenant is a deeply personal relationship between God and his chosen people; it's far more intimate than a contract. But similar to a contract, an agreement of some sort is being formed; something is being pledged. The seriousness of the pledge is symbolized in rituals involving the shedding of *blood*. In Gen 15, there's a scene that might seem quite strange to the modern reader. Abraham cuts animals in half and arranges the pieces, creating a center aisle. Then God passes through the animals. What's this all about? God is saying to Abraham, "If I don't keep my promise to you, may it be done to me as it was to these animals." God uses this powerful image to pledge *himself*, his own faithfulness, to Abraham. Finally, a covenant is a bond in blood *sovereignly administered*. This is not a relationship between equal partners; rather, God is the sovereign Lord, who initiates and establishes the terms of the covenantal relationship.

Genesis 12 reveals what God plans to accomplish through Abraham. God promises that Abraham's descendants will become a great nation; that they will possess the promised land; and that they will be blessed *so that* that they will become a blessing to all nations. Notice how God's promise to Abraham is a promise to restore everything that was lost in Eden:

In the Beginning:
God's people: Adam and Eve.
In God's place: Eden.
Under God's rule: the word of God.
Fulfilling their God-given purpose:
extend Eden to the ends of the earth.
The Promise to Abraham:
God's people: Abraham and his descendants (Israel).
In God's place: the promised land.
Under God's rule: the word of God.
Fulfilling their God-given purpose: blessed so that they will
become a blessing to all nations.

The remainder of Genesis tells us about Abraham's descendants, the patriarchs of God's people: Isaac, Jacob (Israel), and Joseph. Joseph takes the story to Egypt, which brings us to our next major theological theme: exodus.

Exodus: God Rescues His People

The book of Exodus picks up the story some four hundred years after Abraham. Abraham's descendants have multiplied; God's promise to make them a great nation has been partly fulfilled. But a new pharaoh rises to power in Egypt, and he fears the number of Israelites, so he enslaves them. The Israelites cry out to God, and in response to their misery, God calls a man named Moses. God speaks to Moses from a burning bush, reveals his name, Yahweh ("Lord"), and reassures Moses that he remembers the promise made to Abraham. God is faithful; he will indeed deliver his people from Egypt and lead them to the land of promise. And Moses will participate in God's plan; he will be the liberator, the leader of God's people.

God sends Moses to Pharaoh, a tyrant who believes his power is supreme. Pharaoh refuses to let the Israelites leave Egypt, so God sends a series of plagues, showing Pharaoh who truly possesses supreme power. The plagues show us that the God who created all things in the beginning remains in control of all creation. With the final plague, God sends his judgment on all of Egypt, and he provides his people with specific instructions so that they will be spared. They are to take the blood of a lamb and apply it to the door of their homes. God explains, "When I see the blood, I will pass over you, and no plague will befall you to destroy you, when I strike the land of Egypt" (Exod 12:13). This act will profoundly shape the memory of God's people. The event is the basis for the feast of Passover, an annual commemoration of God's mighty acts of deliverance. Finally, Pharaoh releases the Israelites, though he makes one last desperate attempt to stop them as they depart from Egypt. He gathers his army and races after them, but God uses the sea, the greatest symbol of chaotic power in the ancient world, to show that everything is under his control. He parts the Red Sea, providing a path of salvation for his people, and then wields the waves, bringing final judgment on the Egyptians.

Law: God Instructs His People

The rescued Israelites come to Mount Sinai, the same area where God revealed himself to Moses in the burning bush. Now, God reveals himself to the whole nation in thunder and lightning on the mountain, a visible reminder of his power and holiness. Holiness, like covenant, is one of the most important concepts in the biblical story. To say that God is holy is to affirm that he is unique, set apart from all that he has created. Numerous times in the Old Testament, especially in the book of Leviticus, God will say to his people, "Be holy, for I am holy" (e.g., Lev 11:44). Israel is to be different, set apart from the other nations of the world. The Israelites are called to be God's unique people; in other words, they are to reflect God's own character. This is the Genesis mandate restated. Adam and Eve were given the purpose of filling the world with image bearers, people who reflect God's love. Now, Israel is called to reflect God's character, and by reflecting the divine love, mercy, and grace, they will be a blessing to all nations, just as God had promised to Abraham.

At Mount Sinai, God spells out what it means to be holy, what it means to live as his unique people. He gives Israel instructions, commonly referred to as the law, the heart of which are the Ten Commandments. It's very important to notice in Exod 20 that *grace precedes law.* God does not give the law so that by obeying it, Israel will become his people. By sovereignly rescuing Israel from their slavery in Egypt, God has demonstrated that he is their God and they are his chosen people. He now gives them the law so that *as his people*, they will devote themselves to his mission: being a blessing to all nations. Throughout the biblical story, salvation is by grace, and a true experience of God's saving grace leads to holy living. The Ten Commandments, given in Exod 20 and repeated later in Deut 5, define holy living. Only as the Israelites submit their whole lives to God's law will they fulfill their calling to be a blessing to all nations.

Tabernacle: God Dwells with His People

In addition to the giving of the law, God instructs Moses to gather materials to build a complex tent structure known as the tabernacle. In Eden, God dwelled with his people. Since leaving Eden, God has appeared occasionally, such as when he visited Moses in the burning bush or appeared to Israel on Mount Sinai. With the construction of the tabernacle, God will again dwell with his people. The tabernacle becomes the place of worship. Israel is not yet in the land God has promised them; they will be on the move, so for now they need a portable sanctuary. The priests and Levites are the worship leaders, officiating over the sacrifices and offerings of the people.

Much of Leviticus deals with the different kinds of sacrifices and offerings the Israelites brought to the tabernacle. The sacrificial system of the Old Testament was elaborate. It called for daily, weekly, monthly, and occasional offerings. The blood sacrifices all shared the same basic steps. It began with the worshiper bringing the animal, laying his hands on the head of the animal, and then killing it. This was a symbolic transferal of the sins of the worshiper to the animal, and the animal was then killed instead of the worshiper. The sacrifices themselves had no saving power, but they were designed to show the path of salvation. The sacrifices stated emphatically, "For sinful people to be pardoned, something must be punished in their place."

Land: God Provides a Place for His People

God had promised Abraham that his descendants would form a great nation; that they would possess a great land; and that he would bestow his blessing upon them *so that* they would become a blessing to all nations. The Abrahamic covenant was a promise to restore everything that was lost in Eden: God's people, in God's place, under God's rule, fulfilling their God-given purpose. The book of Numbers tells the story of Israel's journey from Mount Sinai to the border of the promised land. Finally, the land of promise is within their reach. They send spies ahead to scout out the land, and they return with both good and bad news: the land is beautiful and fertile, and it would make a perfect homeland for Israel; but, the land is inhabited by powerful people. The report creates fear in the hearts of the Israelites, and their faith in the Lord collapses. They become disgruntled, complaining that God brought them this far only to let them die at the borders of the promised land. In response to their unbelief, God vows that none of this generation will enter the land. The Israelites wander in the wilderness for forty years, until the last of the faithless generation has died.

By the time we come to the book of Joshua, the first faithless generation is gone. Moses, too, has died and has passed the baton of leadership to Joshua. Under Joshua's leadership, Israel will take possession of the promised land, but the story makes it clear that the Lord is not only the one who promised the land but also the one who provides it. In Josh 5, a mysterious figure referred to as the commander of the Lord's army appears to Joshua. Joshua inquires, "Are you for us, or for our adversaries?" The commander says, "No, no, Joshua, you don't understand. I'm not here as some sidekick to support your agenda. I am the captain of this campaign.

I will lead Israel to victory. I will provide the promised land" (see Josh 5:13–15). And indeed, he does. The book of Joshua ends with Israel established in her own land, which represents a major stage in the fulfillment of God's promise to Abraham.

Kingdom: God Rules His People

The book of Judges tells us what happens when Joshua and his generation have died, and the news is not good. A pattern occurs throughout this period of Israel's history: the people rebel against God, God allows another nation to invade, the people repent and cry out to God for help, and God raises up a judge (a military leader) to liberate his people. The final verse summarizes the entire book: "In those days there was no king in Israel. Everyone did what was right in his own eyes" (Judg 21:25).

The books of Samuel, Kings, and Chronicles record the transition from judges to kings. God is the one who chooses the king of Israel. The mortal leader is established as an under-king of the true King. The earthly king was to be the lead covenant keeper, reminding Israel of her true Lord and leading Israel to reflect God's character. The king was God's anointed one—that is, his "messiah."

Saul becomes Israel's first earthly king. David is remembered as Israel's greatest king. In 2 Sam 7, God establishes a covenant with David that echoes the Abrahamic covenant. The new element in the covenant with David is the idea of a kingdom that will endure forever. David's son, Solomon, constructs the temple. Now that the people have settled in the promised land, they no longer need a portable tabernacle. The walls of the temple are painted with palm trees and flowers, recalling the garden-temple of Eden. God's people are once again in God's place under God's rule fulfilling their God-given purpose. But as in Eden, things fall apart. Idolatry pollutes Israel. God had instructed his people, "You shall have no other gods before me" (Exod 20:3; Deut 5:7). "Be holy, for I am holy" (Lev 11:44–45). But, again, they rebelled. Again, they went their own way. After Solomon's death, the kingdom splits into the Northern Kingdom (Israel) and the Southern Kingdom

(Judah). The nation is now divided against itself, and both king-doms are vulnerable.

Exile: God Judges Rebellion

The exile is the most catastrophic event in Israel's story. Rescued from Egypt, placed in the promised land, given the purpose of re-flecting God's character and thereby being a blessing to all nations, Israel instead becomes more and more like the unbelieving nations that surround them. They refuse to serve the Lord, who rescued them and so generously provided for them. And so, just as God banished Adam and Eve from Eden at the beginning of the story, now he allows the nations of Assyria and Babylon to conquer the Northern and Southern Kingdoms. The temple, the place where God dwells with his people, is destroyed. Survivors are deported to foreign lands. Daniel and his friends are some of the best-known examples of this.

The prophetic books of the Old Testament come from the period surrounding the exile. Some prophets were called to warn God's people of the judgment that surely would come upon them if they did not repent. The people refused to heed these warnings. Other prophets ministered to God's people during the time of ex-ile, insisting that exile would not be the end of the story. God's promises to Abraham and David remained. Eventually, the Persian king Cyrus defeated Babylon, and many of God's people were al-lowed to return to their land, where they worked to rebuild what was lost. Prophets continued to announce God's faithfulness, but throughout the entire Old Testament, God's people demonstrated their unfaithfulness.

The Old Testament is a story without an ending. It leaves us with an unresolved dilemma, a riddle that is best summarized in Exod 34:6–7: "The Lord, the Lord, the compassionate and gracious God, slow to anger, abounding in love and faithfulness, maintain-ing love to thousands, and forgiving wickedness, rebellion and sin. Yet he does not leave the guilty unpunished." God is gracious and faithful, yet his people are sinful and unfaithful. God desires to restore everything that was lost in Eden; he has chosen Israel and promised to work through her to bring blessing to all the nations of the world, but Israel continues to rebel. How, then, will God's promise to rescue humanity and restore all of creation be fully and finally realized? To solve this riddle, we must turn to the New Testament.

4

REDEMPTION

In the Gospels, we discover that Jesus Christ is the long-awaited, once-for-all fulfillment of God's promise to redeem his fallen world.

An Intermission of Expectation

IN THE PREVIOUS CHAPTER, we flew through over a thousand years of redemptive history. In case you felt like Falcon trying to keep up with Captain America as he sprinted around the Lincoln Memorial Reflecting Pool, we'll pause for a moment of review—and breath catching. To make sure we're clear on the most important points of the story, let's think about two questions:

What has been broken?

What has been promised?

In the very beginning of the story, the triune God loved his good creation into existence, and he gave humanity everything: fellowship with their Creator and peaceful and purposeful existence in the beautiful place God created for them. In Gen 3, Adam and Eve rebelled against their Creator, and the result of their rebellion was threefold:

A broken relationship with God
(physical and spiritual death).
A broken relationship with each other
(interpersonal conflict).
A broken relationship with creation itself
(cosmic conflict).

But we also saw in Gen 3:15 the first promise of the gospel. As soon as rebellion entered the world of mankind, the hope of redemption was announced. According to Gen 3:15, Eve's offspring would one day defeat the serpent, though at a great cost. The hope of redemption is fleshed out as the story unfolds. In Gen 12, God chooses a man named Abraham, and God reveals that through Abraham, he will work to restore everything that was lost in the beginning, which we've summarized as:

God's people.
In God's place.
Under God's rule.
Fulfilling their God-given purpose.

In the Old Testament chapter of the story, God's promises are partially fulfilled: Israel takes possession of the promised land, but they consistently demonstrate their disloyalty to the God who called them and rescued them from Egypt. Thus, God's people never fulfill their God-given purpose of being a blessing to all nations.

At the end of the Old Testament, God's rebellious people experience the catastrophe of exile: the land of promise is taken, the place of God's presence (the temple) is destroyed, and the people of God are scattered. Eventually, God's people are allowed to return to their homeland. The prophets who minister during this time speak of the Messiah, God's Anointed One, who will one day come to fulfill God's promises in full, to complete his plan to redeem the world.

Between the Old and New Testaments, roughly four hundred years pass. Israel now suffers under imperial Rome. The people of Israel are scattered throughout the Roman Empire and beyond. Among them, there is a fervent longing for God to act. And in this context of expectation, a man named Jesus comes, saying, "The time is fulfilled, and the kingdom of God is at hand; repent and believe in the gospel" (Mark 1:14–15). When Jesus speaks of "the kingdom of God," he means that combination of elements we've seen throughout the story thus far: God's people, in God's place, under God's rule, fulfilling their God-given purpose. Jesus declares that he is *the bringer of the kingdom*. He is the long-awaited one who will fulfill God's promises in full and redeem this fallen world.

The Coming of the King

The four Gospels tell the same story, but with different emphases. The central message of each is the identity and ministry of Jesus Christ. There's a widespread notion that Jesus and Christ are both names, but this is incorrect. Jesus doesn't walk into the room 007 style; order his martini shaken, not stirred; and say, "The name's Christ, Jesus Christ." Christ is not a surname, except perhaps in the old sense in which surnames declared a person's profession: Samuel *Smith* or Thomas *Taylor*. The title "Christ" is a translation of the Greek term *Christos*, which means "the Anointed One, the Messiah." In the Old Testament, certain people were anointed as a way of being set apart for a special service. King David is often referred to as "the anointed of God." Matthew begins his Gospel by referring to Jesus as the "son of David," recalling the promise made to David, Israel's great king, that one day a far greater king would come. Long ago, God made a promise to David that one of his descendants would rule forever (2 Sam 7). Jesus is the fulfillment of this promise. He's also the "son of Abraham," the fulfillment of the promise recorded in Gen 12: that through Abraham, all the nations of the earth would be blessed. Matthew 1:1 declares that Jesus is the Messiah, the Savior-King promised within the pages of the Old Testament, who has come to establish a worldwide and everlasting kingdom.

John begins his Gospel with a connection to Gen 1:1: "In the beginning, God created the heavens and the earth." John says, "In the beginning was the Word," a reference to Jesus, the ultimate message of God. He goes on to say that "the Word was God" (John 1:1). So, this Jesus is not merely the human son of David, the son of Abraham; he is also the Son of God, meaning that he shares the nature of God the Father. Jesus is fully human and fully divine. This is his true identity, and his identity reveals his ministry: Jesus, the God-Man, comes to restore the broken relationship between God and humanity. In Jesus, God will again dwell with his people. A more literal translation of the Greek text in John 1:14 is "And the Word became flesh and *tabernacled* among us" (my translation). In the Old Testament, the tabernacle and then the temple represented the dwelling of God among his people. The presence of God demonstrated that the promised land was not merely living space but the setting for a relationship between God and humanity. Jesus has come to restore this relationship once and for all.

Jesus' earthly parents are Mary and Joseph. He is born in the city of Bethlehem, the birthplace of David. He grows up in Nazareth with his siblings. We know very few details from the period between Jesus' birth and the events that immediately precede his public ministry. Preparing the way for Jesus' public ministry is his cousin, a man named John, the Baptizer. John's preparatory message is that God's people must repent and be baptized in water. He baptizes people in the Jordan River, the place where Israel entered the promised land more than a thousand years earlier. John's baptism in this particular place signals a new beginning for God's people, a cleansing from sin. One day, a crowd comes to John to be baptized, and Jesus is among them. Jesus doesn't need to be cleansed from sin, but he comes to identify himself with God's people. As he is baptized, the Holy Spirit comes upon him and the Father declares that Jesus is indeed the Anointed One who will bring the kingdom of God.

Jesus will succeed where God's people of the past have failed. This is demonstrated in Jesus' own wilderness experience, which follows his baptism. In the wilderness, Jesus is tempted by Satan, just as Adam and Eve were tempted in Eden. But where the first Adam succumbed to the temptation and rebelled against his Creator, Jesus, who elsewhere is called "the last Adam" (1 Cor 15:45), stands firm in the face of temptation. Jesus' forty days in the wilderness recall the forty years Israel wandered in the wilderness until the faithless generation passed away. The temptation in the wilderness shows us that where Adam and Israel were unfaithful, Jesus will be faithful.

Mark 1 provides the basic outline of Jesus' public ministry. As we've seen, Jesus comes saying, "The time is fulfilled, and the kingdom of God is at hand" (Mark 1:14-15). During the three years of his public ministry, Jesus devotes himself to three things: he forms a kingdom community; he reveals the kingdom through miracles; and he explains the kingdom through sermons and stories.

Matthew's Gospel in particular highlights the fact that Jesus' earliest efforts to establish a community of followers takes place primarily within Israel. Redemption will begin with the chosen people of Israel, but it will not be limited to them. The community of disciples begins to form as Jesus declares the good news of the kingdom and calls for people to respond with repentance and faith. Some of Jesus' disciples follow him while remaining in their own villages and homes. Others are called to leave everything behind and travel full-time with him. This latter group becomes known as the apostles. Jesus selects twelve apostles, representing the twelve tribes of Israel. The apostles minister with Jesus: they watch him, listen to his teaching, and come to know his way of life, and eventually, they will be sent out to share the message of Jesus with the world. To have communion with Jesus is to share in his mission. Jesus also welcomes tax collectors, prostitutes, the poor, and the sick—the least, the last, and the lost of society. He shares meals with these individuals as a way of showing that, though they are outcasts to many, they are friends of the King.

Jesus also performs a number of miracles: he heals the sick, drives out dark spiritual forces, shows his control over the powers of nature, and even causes death to give back the life it claimed. These mighty works are signs that reveal who Jesus is and what he has come to accomplish. The miracles are like windows through which we get a glimpse of the new creation, fully redeemed, finally rid of the pain, conflict, and death that came into the world as a result of humanity's rebellion.

In addition to these mighty works, Jesus teaches his followers about the kingdom. The Sermon on the Mount is the most well known example of Jesus' instruction to his disciples. His teaching also took the form of stories. Throughout his public ministry, Jesus told more than forty parables. These parables reveal many truths about the kingdom of God, and one of the most shocking is that the kingdom will not come all at once. The popular understanding among Jews of the day was that the Anointed One, the Messiah, would be God's agent for immediate reform and restoration, a great Warrior-King who would deal swiftly with all oppressors and liberate God's people forever. Jesus is indeed the Messiah; he fulfills all Old Testament expectations, but he does so in such a surprising way that no one could have fully predicted the way he would bring in the kingdom.

The Death of the King

In Mark 14, Jesus dramatizes the climactic event of his earthly ministry, his death. He had foretold his death on other occasions, and his disciples had failed to understand this most critical part of the kingdom mission. Peter once responded to Jesus with sharp criticism: "You're the Anointed One, the Messiah. You cannot die; you've come to rescue us!" (see Mark 8:31–33). In Mark 14, Jesus declares that *death will be the path to deliverance*. This had been foreshadowed centuries ago, in the event that Jesus and his disciples now gathered to commemorate, the exodus. The Passover meal was part of the annual commemoration of God's mighty acts of deliverance during the days of Moses (Exod 12). A lamb was slaughtered and its blood applied to the door of the home; the lamb died, and the Israelites were spared from judgment and rescued from their slavery in Egypt. The entire Old Testament sacrificial system pointed forward to the reality that Jesus reveals here. The blood of animals could never cope with the problems of humanity (Heb 10:4). The animal sacrifices had no saving power;

they merely showed the path of salvation. At this last meal with his disciples, Jesus announces that his blood will establish a new covenant. Covenant, as we learned from the Old Testament, is the language of relationship. Jesus came to form a new relationship between God and man, because the previous relationship had been destroyed by rebellion. All that was broken in the very beginning finds healing in Jesus. He is the "the Lamb of God, who takes away the sin of the world" (John 1:29). It is his death on the cross that accomplishes the redemption of this fallen world.

All four Gospel writers describe Jesus' death in great detail. His crucifixion took place at Golgotha, "Place of a Skull" (Matt 27:33). We don't know how Golgotha acquired its name. Maybe it was because this was a popular site for Roman executions. Perhaps it was because there were numerous tombs nearby. Certainly, it was a place that reeked of death. Jesus began his journey to the Skull (Luke 23:33) carrying his cross, a beam that would have weighed at least thirty or forty pounds. The walk was long for a man who had endured a scourging, an excruciating punishment involving a leather whip with pieces of lead or bone attached to its ends. Weak from the loss of blood, Jesus collapsed, so the soldiers grabbed a man from the crowd and forced him to carry the cross the remainder of the way. When they arrived at Golgotha, a number of things could have happened. The Romans employed a number of different crucifixion techniques, each of them horrific. Crucifixion was a savagely cruel way of eliminating undesirables, a form of execution that brought agony and the maximum amount of humiliation before death. Classical Roman authors were reluctant to write of crucifixion in any detail, presumably because of its gruesome nature. Once tied or nailed to the cross, the victim found it very difficult to breath, due to the strain placed on the chest by the weight of the body. To prolong the suffering, Roman executioners would sometimes place a small wooden seat on the upright beam of the cross, allowing the victim to struggle for air a little longer. Eventually, the person would die from exhaustion, unable to breath. This is what happened to Jesus. After enduring the torment for many hours, he took his last breath. At this exact moment, back in the city and deep within the temple itself, something strange happened. The curtain inside the temple that separated the place of God's presence from the people was torn from top to bottom, signaling a new beginning. The death of Jesus opened the way between God and man.

The Victory of the King

Resurrection of the dead sounds impossible, doesn't it? And it is impossible. Impossible for man. Jesus' resurrection is the ultimate revelation of his identity. This is not a mere man. It can't be. Because men don't come back from the dead. But this man conquered death. He took the most permanent thing imaginable—death—and he made it temporary. The Gospels tell us about specific people who encountered the risen Son of God. They saw him with their own eyes and even touched his wounds. Jesus didn't seep out of the tomb as a spirit or ghost. He emerged from the grave with a new body, and this marks the beginning of the new creation.

We have a tendency to underestimate the gospel. To understand what I mean, we must return to the question with which we began the chapter: What has been broken? The answer is our relationship with God, with each other, and with creation itself. We tend to reduce the gospel to a message about "forgiveness of sins" and "going to heaven when I die." But if this is all there is to the gospel, then Jesus doesn't really do anything about racism and injustice, viruses and cancer, and all the other forms of brokenness in the world. Certainly, it's true that in dying, Jesus takes on the judgment for our rebellion, and through faith in him, we are forgiven of our sins and our fellowship with our Creator is forever restored. But the gospel is much bigger than this. The entire world is broken. And Jesus came to redeem it all. In rising from the dead, Jesus launches the new creation, the new world. Remember the miracles Jesus performed. The windows through which we get a glimpse of the new creation—fully redeemed; finally rid of the pain, conflict, and death that came as a result of humanity's rebellion. Jesus' resurrection is the beginning of this new creation. But remember also the parables of the kingdom. Jesus is the bringer of the kingdom of God, but the kingdom *will not come all at once*. Not long after Jesus is raised, he returns to heaven, with the promise that he will one day return to complete the transformation of his creation. In the meantime, he says to his people: "Go and make disciples of all nations" (Matt 28:19). The language echoes the promise to Abraham that his descendants would be a blessing *to all nations*. It also recalls the mandate first given in Eden: *fill the world* with image bearers. Now that Jesus has accomplished the redemption of his people, he will empower them to fulfill their God-given purpose. He will empower us for his mission until the day of his return.

5

MISSION

Jesus is the bringer of the kingdom of God, but the kingdom does not arrive all at once. In the interim between Jesus' first and second comings, he empowers his people to bear witness to him throughout the world.

Anticipated, Accomplished, Applied, and Announced

WE LONG TO BE part of a story. This longing is evident in our children, especially. As I was writing this very chapter, my youngest son paid me two visits in my home study: first, dressed as Iron Man, and a matter of moments later, as Captain Barbosa! Deep down, we all long to be part of some great story. As followers of Jesus, we are not just *storytellers*; we are *story dwellers*, characters within the great story of the redemption of the world. We have an important part to play within this story, though we are not the *hero* of the story. We're *heralds*. A herald is a message carrier. In J. K. Rowlings's Harry Potter series, Hagrid is the herald. Far from the hero of the story, Hagrid is unpolished, unintelligent, altogether unimpressive. But he's the one who delivers the life-changing, identity- and story-altering message to young Harry Potter in *Harry Potter and the Sorcerer's Stone*: "You're a wizard, Harry." In the story of redemption, we are the heralds; Jesus is the hero.

In the first several chapters of this book, we looked at what we might call the backstory of our hero. We journeyed through the Old Testament. This was a challenging trek for many of us, perhaps because we've never thought deeply about how the Old and New Testaments fit together to form one story. I've tried to help us see that if we don't have at least a basic sense of the backstory (i.e., the Old Testament), then we cannot fully understand everything the hero of the story, Jesus, came to accomplish *for* us and *through* us. As Mark Dever puts it, the Old Testament is about *promises made*, and the New Testament is about *promises kept*. They belong together, like peanut butter and jelly, bacon and eggs, chips and salsa, chicken and waffles—that last one's debatable.

In the previous chapter, we focused on the identity and ministry of Jesus, and we discovered that Jesus came to restore everything that was broken in the beginning:

Our relationship with God.

Our relationship with others.

Our relationship with creation itself.

Jesus does this by being the God-Man and dying in the place of rebels—that's you and me—and then rising from the dead, conquering the powers of sin and death, and launching the new creation. Jesus has *accomplished* the redemption of his broken world, but—and this is important—what Jesus has *accomplished* for us is not *applied* to us until we place our faith in him, until we repent and believe in the gospel.

To believe in Jesus is to become a herald in his story, to participate in his plan for the world. Jesus is the bringer of the kingdom of God:

God's people.

In God's place.

Under God's rule.

Fulfilling their God-given purpose.

But Jesus will come to this earth *twice*; thus, the kingdom does not arrive all at *once*. At the beginning of the book of Acts, the disciples come to the risen Jesus and ask, "Lord, will you at this time restore the kingdom to Israel?" (Acts 1:6). Remember that the popular understanding among Jews of Jesus' day was that the Anointed One, the Messiah, would be God's agent for immediate restoration, a great Warrior-King who would deal swiftly with all oppressors and liberate God's people forever. What the disciples are getting at is this: "Hey Jesus, are you gonna exercise your power, wipe out our Roman oppressors, and make Israel great? Has the kingdom of God finally arrived?" In essence, Jesus' answer is "Yes, the kingdom has arrived, but not yet in full. You've got work to do." The kingdom will come in fullness as Jesus works through the community of his followers.

A Spirit-Filled Community

In Acts 1, the risen Jesus appears to his disciples and tells them to wait in Jerusalem for the promised Holy Spirit, the empowering presence of God. In Acts 2, Jesus has ascended to heaven, and the disciples are camping out, waiting, just as Jesus had commanded them. The occasion is the day of Pentecost, a Jewish holiday. Pentecost was originally a harvest festival (Exod 23:16), but in time, it became a day to commemorate the giving of the law at Mount Sinai. Because it was the day of Pentecost, thousands of Jewish pilgrims from all over the known world were gathered in Jerusalem.

Three very strange things happened on that day. First, "there came from heaven a sound like a mighty rushing wind, and it filled the house where [the disciples] were sitting" (Acts 2:2). This is a figure of speech: it's not an actual hurricane but a sound *like* a mighty wind. Luke is describing the descent of the Holy Spirit in terms that are easily understandable. It sounds like a blustery day on the beach. Second, "divided tongues as of fire appeared to [the disciples] and rested on each one of them" (Acts 2:3). What does this mean? In the Old Testament, wind and fire often accompany the presence of God. In Exodus, when God descends to Mount

Sinai to meet with his people and to give them the law, how is the divine presence described? Storm and fire. Or think about Exod 3, when God calls Moses. What does Moses see? A burning bush. In the Old Testament, fire symbolizes the presence of God. So what does it mean here in Acts 2 when fire rests on each of the disciples? It means that every believer is now a burning bush. It means that God is present *with* and *in* his people. The Old Testament prophets promised not only that the Messiah would come but also that the Spirit would come to transform and empower God's people. Ezekiel summarizes this promise: "And I will put my Spirit in you and move you to follow my decrees and be careful to keep my laws" (Ezek 36:27 NIV). How is it that this community of Christ followers will be capable of fulfilling their God-given purpose where God's people of the past have so frequently failed? This community of believers has the empowering presence of God *within* them.

Third, according to Acts 2:4, "they were all filled with the Holy Spirit and began to speak in other tongues as the Spirit gave them utterance." The disciples are filled with the Spirit, and the result is some type of miraculous speech. "Tongues" is a misleading translation here. "Tongues" is often defined as a type of speech or prayer that is unintelligible to people, understood only by God. But this is not what we find in Acts 2. The context clarifies the gift that comes to the disciples: this is a miracle of speaking unlearned languages. If you've ever learned a new language, you know that it's hard work. I remember when I first learned Hebrew and Greek in seminary. I drilled myself with flash cards every morning. I had a mini dry-erase board that I carried throughout the day to write noun and verb endings. In Acts 2, the disciples don't need flash cards or dry-erase boards. Suddenly, instantly, they are able to speak languages they've never spoken before. And what do they speak about? Luke tells us that they speak about "the mighty works of God." They declare the gospel, and Jews from all over the world are able to understand the message. For a moment, Babel is reversed. Do you remember the story from Gen 10? Because of humanity's prideful endeavors, God came down and brought division of languages and confusion. Here in Acts 2, God comes down and brings unity and clarity. What does this miracle of unlearned languages mean? It means that God's desire is for the gospel to go to all nations, for people of every language to know the message of the mighty works of God, what God has done for us and for all of creation in Jesus Christ. This is not a message for Israel only; it's a universal message, a global hope.

A Witnessing Community

If we backtrack to Acts 1:8, we find the road map for the church's witness. Before Jesus returns to heaven, he tells his followers to wait for the promised empowering presence. Once the Spirit arrives, Jesus says, "You will be my witnesses in Jerusalem and in all Judea and Samaria, and to the end of the earth." The community's witness launches in their current location; it reaches the surrounding regions; and finally, it extends to the end of the earth. Their God-given purpose is to bear witness to the redeeming work of Jesus Christ in every location, crossing all geographical, ethnic, and socioeconomic boundaries.

In his classic book *Evangelism in the Early Church*, Michael Green provides a detailed account of the evangelistic methods of the early Christian community. Basically, we find three types of witnessing throughout the book of Acts. The first is public proclamation. The work of preaching and teaching occurs throughout Acts in a variety of settings and before an array of audiences. As soon as the Spirit descends to indwell believers, Peter starts preaching (Acts 2:14–36). This, in fact, is the first Christian sermon, and like all the sermons recorded in Acts, it's Christ centered in its content.

Later in Acts, we read about the conversion of a man named Saul of Tarsus, who becomes known as the apostle Paul, the greatest missionary of all time. Paul took three lengthy missionary journeys, traveling over fifteen thousand miles. What made Paul such a great missionary was not just the distance he covered but the principle he introduced, a principle that missiologists today refer to as *contextualization*. The principle is simply this: the most effective way to share Christ-centered content is to analyze your particular audience and then adapt the communication of the gospel to the audience without altering the gospel itself. In the field of education, there's a saying: "To teach math to Johnny, you need to know both math and Johnny." In the field of evangelism and missions, we could say, "To share the gospel with Johnny, we need to know both the gospel and Johnny." Paul was so effective at sharing the gospel because he didn't have a one-size-fits-all approach. He didn't take an evangelism class at his local church, memorize a script, and then bounce from one city to the next spewing the script on anyone within spewing distance. A careful reading of Acts reveals that Paul had *many ways* of communicating the *one gospel*, and his audience dictated his approach.

The second type of witnessing we find in Acts, according to Green, is household evangelism. For the first 150-plus years, there were no church buildings, so homes were one of the primary tools for the spread of the gospel. The earliest Christians used their homes in multiple ways. They often decorated the outside of their homes with mosaics and symbols that were subtle enough to invite questions from neighbors, which might then lead to conversations about the faith. Groups of Christians gathered in homes for worship and teaching, prayer meetings, and Communion. And family discipleship took place in the home. Typically, when the father of the family became a Christian, the entire household would follow his lead. The same is true roughly two thousand years later. According to Larry Alex Taunton in *The Faith of Christopher Hitchens*, modern studies have shown that when a mother converts to Christianity, 17 percent of the time, the children also convert. When a father converts to Christianity, 93 percent of the time, the children also convert.

In addition to public proclamation and household evangelism, Green demonstrates that personal encounters—one-on-one spiritual conversations—played a vital role in the spread of the gospel. In Acts 8, a Jewish man named Philip is led to an Ethiopian eunuch, a black-skinned, sexually altered man. These two men could not have been more different, and yet as Philip shares the gospel with the Ethiopian and he believes, the two become brothers in Christ, partners in the purpose of announcing King Jesus to the world. According to early Christian writers like Irenaeus, this eunuch became the first Christian missionary to Ethiopia. As important as pastors and missionaries were in the early church, Michael Green concludes that the key players in the expansion of Christianity appear not to have been the professionals but men and women with "secular" careers who spoke of their faith to those they met in everyday life.

A Giving Community

The early Christian community both shared the truth and showed the love of Jesus. Words of truth and acts of service. They displayed the gospel through their generosity. Acts 4 is a beautiful example of this: landowners selling their property in order to give to the needy people around them. And this is not the only example of such radical generosity. The Roman emperor Julian had an interesting "complaint" about early Christians which Finley Hooper and Matthew Schwartz quote in *Roman Letters*: "[They] support not only their own poor but ours as well . . . [;] all men see that our people lack aid from us." In other words, "Those ridiculously generous Christians are making us look like we do nothing to care for the poor!" This radical generosity was a powerful witness to the love of God and the life-changing power of the gospel.

Passages like Acts 4 challenge us, the modern expression of this same community, to turn from our materialism, our desire to acquire. One of Leo Tolstoy's most famous short stories is entitled "How Much Land Does a Man Need?" The main character of the story is a man named Pakhom, who believes that the secret to the good life is more land. "My only problem in life," Pakhom says, "is that I don't have enough land. Give me enough of that and I'd fear no one—not even the Devil himself!" But the Devil had been listening in: "Good!" he thought. "I'll have a little game with you. I shall see that you have plenty of land and that way I'll get you in my clutches!"

As the story unfolds, Pakhom encounters opportunity after opportunity to purchase land. Each time, his purchase brings him great joy—at first. But the joy of the good life soon gives way to thoughts of the better life that could be realized somewhere else. One day, Pakhom encounters a merchant who tells him of the far-off land of the Bashkirs, where he can purchase thousands of acres for the tiniest sum. Without delay, Pakhom says goodbye to his wife, grabs his workman, and heads straight to the land of the Bashkirs. There, he meets the elder, who tells him that the price of land is "a thousand roubles a day." Pakhom is confused, so the elder explains: "However much land you can walk round in one day will be yours. And the price is the same: a thousand roubles. But there's one condition: you must return to your starting-point by sunset." Pakhom can't believe what he is hearing. What an incredible opportunity! "A man can walk round a lot of land in a day!" The next day, Pakhom starts walking, marking all the land he can. And the further he travels, the better the land gets. When his body begins to feel tired, he keeps walking, coaching himself, "A moment's pain can be a lifetime's gain." Finally, he decides that he has journeyed far enough, so he turns around and heads for the starting point, but on the way back, Pakhom finds the going tough. The heat of the day has exhausted him. His legs are giving out. He is so thirsty, so tired, but he can't rest. "I'll never get back by sunset," he thinks. His fear makes him only more breathless. On he runs, his clothes soaked, his throat parched. In the distance, he sees the starting point. He takes a deep breath and runs with all the energy he has left, diving and arriving at the starting point just before the sun goes down. The Bashkirs are there to cheer for him. "Well done!" the elder says. "That's a lot of land you've earned yourself." Pakhom's workman runs to his master's side to help him stand on his feet so he can join the celebration. But Pakhom is dead. The venture has claimed his life. And his workman buries him in the land that is the product of his greed.

Tolstoy and Luke, the writer of Acts, tell two very different stories: one a tale of life-claiming greed; the other a tale of life-changing generosity. As the early Christian community proclaimed the good news of Jesus and displayed radical generosity, their entire world was changed. According to New Testament scholar Larry Hurtado in his book *Destroyer of the Gods*, there were about one thousand Christians in 40 AD, about seven to ten thousand by 100 AD, about two hundred thousand by 200 AD, and more than five million by 300 AD. The final word in the Greek text of the book of Acts is best translated as "unhindered" or "unstoppable." The spread of the gospel is "unstoppable." Jesus himself said, "I will build my church" (Matt 16:18). Jesus is bringing his kingdom right now. He is working *in* and *through* his people to change the world. And one day, King Jesus will return to complete his plan for his creation.

6

NEW CREATION

When we don't have at least a basic understanding of the backstory (the Old Testament), we can't fully understand everything the hero of the story (Jesus) came to accomplish for us, and the final result is an underestimation of the Christian hope, a misunderstanding of the end of the story.

The Cosmic Redeemer

THROUGHOUT THIS BOOK, I have sought to tell the story of Scripture, the one great story that runs from Genesis to Revelation. In previous chapters, we've learned that if we don't have at least a basic sense of the backstory (i.e., the Old Testament), then we cannot fully understand everything the hero of the story (Jesus) came to accomplish. In this final chapter, we'll add to this: If we don't have at least a basic understanding of the backstory, then we can't fully understand everything the hero of the story came to accomplish, and the final result will be an underestimation of the Christian hope, a misunderstanding of the end of the story. Jesus is the bringer of the kingdom of God, and Jesus will come to this earth *twice*; thus, the kingdom does not arrive all at *once*. The kingdom will come in fullness as the risen and ascended Jesus works through the community of his followers until the day of his return. When Jesus returns, he will complete his plan for the world. And his plan involves a final place. But what is this final place? What is our ultimate hope?

An old hymn suggests, "This world is not my home, I'm just a passing through." I suggest, instead, that "*heaven* is not my home, I'm just a passing through." We must remember that Jesus came to restore everything that was broken in the beginning:

Our relationship with God.

Our relationship with others.

Our relationship with creation itself.

Jesus is the *cosmic Redeemer*. He will return to complete his plan for *the world*. And this means that heaven is not the final resting place or the ultimate hope of the Christ follower. When a believer passes away, he or she goes immediately into the presence of Jesus in heaven. Heaven is *better* than this world in its current, corrupted form; but heaven is not *best*. Heaven is a place of restful waiting. When King Jesus returns, the final place for God's people will be formed, and it will not be an ethereal place somewhere up there but a physical place right here. There will be a solidity to eternity. Fashioned from the dust of the earth (Gen 2:7), earthly in the end we shall be.

Reading Revelation Responsibly

If this is shocking news to you, perhaps it's because you haven't spent enough time with the final book of the Bible, Revelation. I don't blame you. Revelation is full of freaky stuff. The first thing we need to get straight is the title of the book: it's Revelation, not Revelation*s*. I feel a bit like Hermione Granger in *Harry Potter and the Sorcerer's Stone* ("It's leviOsa, not levioSA!"), but we do need to know the title of the book we're studying. Revelation is a work of life-altering theology, but its literary form frightens many people away. Most Christians can pick up John's Gospel or Paul's Letter to the Philippians and immediately make pretty good sense of what they're reading. Then these same people turn to Revelation, and they encounter colored horses, a dragon, wicked beasts, and a prostitute. They begin to wonder, "Am I still reading the Bible? Or am I watching *Cowboys & Aliens?*"

A responsible reading of Revelation begins with an understanding of the genre of the book. To identify the genre of a book is to ask the question "*What* am I reading? What type of literature is this?" Identifying the type of literature we're reading is crucial. If you don't believe me, run to Barnes & Noble this afternoon, pick up a book of Caribbean recipes, and then try to use the book to find your way from Barbados to St. Bart's. You'll end up doubly disappointed: hungry and lost. Revelation is apocalyptic literature. When we hear the word "apocalypse," we think of some very unfortunate event, an episode involving mass destruction. In the Marvel show *Loki*, the Variant hides in the apocalypses of the time line. While *Loki* is indeed a great show, we need to set aside this definition. In the first century, the word "apocalypse" referred not to an unfortunate event but to an unveiling of something. The first words of the book of Revelation are "the unveiling [*apokalypsis*] of Jesus Christ" (Rev 1:1, my translation).

The goal of apocalyptic literature is to give us an alternative reading of reality. It changes our perception of the world in which we live. Revelation is like the Reality Stone (let the Marvel fan understand). Its power changes our perception of everything around us, but in this case, it shows us the *true* reality. Revelation reveals that things are not as they seem. There is more to reality than meets the eye.

How does apocalyptic literature accomplish its goal? How does Revelation change our perception? By creating a symbolic world which we enter into so fully that it changes the way we see and experience the world around us. Something similar happens when we become engrossed in an epic film. For those few hours, we enter the world of the film, and what we experience within that world causes us to see the world around us differently; it changes our perspective and awakens our passion. We emerge from the world of Middle-earth with a sense that, no matter how small and unlikely a character we might be, we can fight against the darkness of our day. This is how Revelation works on us, how it changes our perspective of the world: by drawing us into its symbolic world.

Symbolic is a key word. A defining feature of apocalyptic literature is its use of symbols, bizarre images that stand for something else. Many of us have been taught the maxim "Interpret literally except when we are forced to interpret symbolically." Those who interpret Revelation literally are waiting for the day when a sea monster, an earth monster, and a dragon will appear on the earth, like a scene from *Pacific Rim* or *Godzilla*. But this is to disregard the genre of the book. Apocalyptic literature uses symbols. The Lamb is not a literal lamb—not a fluffy, four-legged animal; it's a symbol for Jesus, the one slain for our sins. The dragon is not a literal dragon—not a medieval, fire-breathing monster; it's a symbol for Satan, the primeval, lie-breathing leader of all rebellion against God and his people.

Our Otherworldly Adversary

While I was working on this book, Mike Cosper's popular podcast *The Rise and Fall of Mars Hill* was being produced. One of the episodes begins with the fascinating story of the Cottingley Fairies. One summer's day in 1917, in a village called Cottingley in England, two cousins named Frances and Elsie returned home soaking wet from playing in a creek. Their family scolded them for ruining their clothes, but the young girls had an excuse. It wasn't their fault, they explained; the fairies had lured them into the muddy water. When the mothers rolled their eyes, Francis and Elsie decided to prove it. They borrowed Elsie's father's camera and returned to the creek. When they came back, her father developed the photographic plates. In the first picture, he saw little Francis surrounded by four white fairies. In the coming weeks, they'd take more photos, all of them showing the girls surrounded by fairies. Elsie's father knew enough about photography (and enough about his daughter's impish behavior) to be skeptical. But Elsie's mother believed the story. She took the photos to the Theosophical Society, an organization devoted to the study of world religions, philosophy, science, and the supernatural. At this point, the story went as viral as something could go in those days. By 1920, the Cottingley Fairies had become the talk of London, inviting comment from some of the most brilliant minds of the day. One author wrote of the fairies: "The recognition of their existence will jolt the material twentieth-century mind out of its heavy ruts in the mud and will make it admit that there is a glamour and a mystery to life." That author was Sir Arthur Conan Doyle, the creator of the famous literary character Sherlock Holmes. The story of the Cottingley Fairies persisted for over forty years. In 1966, Elsie was interviewed and, for the first time, explained that the fairies were figments of her imagination, though she refused to elaborate. It wasn't until 1983, sixty-six years after the first picture was taken, that Elsie and Francis together acknowledged that the photographs were fake. Francis said, "I never even thought of it being a fraud. It was just Elsie and I having a bit of fun . . . . People often say to me, 'Don't you feel ashamed that you've made all these poor people look like fools? They believed in you.' But I don't [feel ashamed] because they wanted to believe."

People want to believe that there is more to this world than meets the eye, more than what we consider normal, or natural. I colead a small group of dudes mostly in their thirties and forties. Theology on Tap, we call ourselves. It's a motley crew. Different church backgrounds and life experiences, various vocations: we have Lieutenant Dan, Captain Kirk (the same one from the introduction), fix-anything Ron, break-you-with-one-punch Earl, and several others. We've met together for years, and every semester, somehow, we end up discussing ghosts, or aliens, or whether an alien can come back as a ghost. Somebody should make a movie about that.

The Bible doesn't specifically address subjects like aliens or fairies. It does, however, teach us that we are not alone in the universe. There *is* a supernatural, or spiritual, realm and many spiritual beings, including our most powerful enemy. This otherworldly adversary first surfaced in the biblical story back in Gen 3. Revelation clarifies that the seductive serpent from the garden of Eden is Satan, the one who has been planting doubt, breathing lies, and wreaking havoc since the very beginning of the world. Since 9/11 and the sight of the burning towers, the problem of the existence of evil has become inescapable. The human will can do unfathomably wicked things. Why? *Star Wars* is on the right track with its idea of a "Force" behind all evil. But according to the true story of the universe, the "Force" is a he. Revelation 12:9 describes him as "the great dragon . . . that ancient serpent, who is called the devil and Satan." Throughout the Bible, and in Revelation in particular, Satan is pictured as the supreme (but not sovereign) otherworldly adversary, a spiritual being hell-bent on leading humanity away from the good and loving God, who created us. But get this: according to the New Testament, Satan has already been defeated.

Jesus' coming to earth, his cross, and his coming to life again defeated the dragon. John tells us in his first letter: "The reason the Son of God appeared was to destroy the works of the devil" (1 John 3:8). We see signs of this mission throughout the Gospels. Just before Jesus launches his public ministry, he goes into the wilderness, where he resists the temptations of Satan. The dragon breathes his lies, just as he did with Adam at the very beginning of the biblical story. Where Adam succumbed to the temptation, Jesus overcomes. All throughout his earthly ministry, Jesus demonstrates his power over Satanic forces. When you read the Gospels, you might get the impression that one out of every three people in the ancient world was demonized. There seem to be demons everywhere. Have you ever wondered what that's all about? The unparalleled demonic manifestations are a sign of Satan fighting—desperately!—for his kingdom against Jesus' attack on it. Jesus' ability to resist Satan's temptations, his power to liberate people from demonic oppression: all of this points to what Jesus came to accomplish. All of it points to what he *did* accomplish at the cross. In language we find elsewhere in the New Testament, the cross "cancels the record of debt that stood against us," thereby "disarming" the dragon (Col 2:14–15). The dragon has been decisively defeated. And on the day of Jesus' return, the dragon will be destroyed.

The Final Battle

Throughout the pages of the New Testament, we find the promise of Jesus' return to the earth. In Matt 24, Jesus himself says, "Concerning that day and hour no one knows . . . . Therefore you must also be ready, for the Son of Man is coming at an hour you do not expect" (Matt 24:36, 44). Jesus is scheduled for arrival, but not in the same way the Amazon package is scheduled for arrival at your house. We don't have a tracking number for Jesus. We know he's coming, but we don't know when. And so, we must be ready today and remain ready each day. In Acts 1, the crucified and risen Jesus promises his disciples the power of the Holy Spirit, and then he ascends into heaven. The disciples saw it: "As they were looking on, he [Jesus] was lifted up, and a cloud took him out of their sight" (Acts 1:9). Then angels appear, dressed in white, with a message: "Why do you stand looking into heaven? Jesus will come again in the same way you saw him go" (Acts 1:11).

In Rev 19, we're transported forward in time to the day of which the white messengers spoke, the day of the second coming of Jesus, the arrival of the White Rider. Dust off your DVDs (for those who still have them) or rent *The Lord of the Rings: The Two Towers*. At the end of the film is one of the great battle scenes of movie history, the Battle of Helm's Deep. The evil army has surrounded and now invaded the fortress. Aragorn and Theoden ride out to meet the enemy. But they're outnumbered. Until they look to the mountain, where they see the White Rider, shining like the sun. Gandalf the White comes to their aid, just as he had promised. Down the mountain he and his massive army ride, so bright they blind the enemy, so strong they shatter the front line. The same Jesus who entered the world by being born among the animals in Bethlehem, who entered Jerusalem on a donkey—a symbol of peace—will reenter the world on a horse—a symbol of war. Jesus will come as the Warrior who will end all wars. That the horse is white signifies that its rider is pure; so is the judgment he brings. This is the righteous Warrior, the just Judge.

Most intriguing is what the Rider wears: "a robe dipped in blood" (Rev 19:13). This Rider is on his way to the final battle—it hasn't yet begun—and already he's bloody. The blood on his robe is his own. The White Rider is the Lamb who was slain, who "ransomed people for God from every tribe and language and people and nation" (Rev 5:9). All who in faith follow him have no need to fear his judgment. He wears the robe that declares in color, "Your sin has been dealt with."

This Rider is known by many names. One is "the Word of God" (Rev 19:13). John uses this phrase in his Gospel: "In the beginning was the Word, and the Word was *with* God, and the Word *was* God" (John 1:1). This Rider is the eternal Son of God, the one present and active at the beginning of creation. Additionally, we're told: "from his mouth comes a sharp sword" (Rev 19:15). The Rider's weapon is his word. It's the only weapon he needs to destroy the dragon. The one who in the beginning was powerful enough to speak the earth into existence in the end is powerful enough to speak evil into extinction. The final battle is the never-fought battle. Jesus returns. Speaks. And fire consumes the armies of darkness (Rev 20:9–10). Mic drop of all mic drops.

The New Physical World

Following the last battle and final judgment, we get a glimpse of the ultimate hope of the Christ follower. In Rev 21:1, John writes, "Then I saw a new heaven and a new earth, for the first heaven and the first earth had passed away." Notice the resurrection pattern: the first creation "passes away" and is replaced by "a new heaven and a new earth." Jesus himself establishes this resurrection pattern. Jesus died and was raised. Jesus says to us, "I am the resurrection and the life. Those who believe in me, even though they die, they will live" (John 11:25). And now we see in Rev 21 that when Jesus returns, the first creation will pass away and a new creation will emerge. Those who in faith follow Jesus will receive resurrection bodies and will live forever in the resurrected world, the world finally healed of all the brokenness that has existed from the time of Adam and Eve's rebellion. Remember that it's not just *people* who are in need of redemption but also the whole *planet*.

What will this new world be like? Jesus himself establishes the resurrection pattern, so we must first look to Jesus as we attempt to answer this question. Was Jesus' resurrection body like or unlike his pre-resurrection body? Both. People still recognized him. He ate solid food. He communicated the same way. Many things were the same. But some things were different. After his resurrection, it seems that Jesus was able to disappear and reappear at will and pass through locked doors (John 20). So, we have to say that Jesus' resurrection body was both *like* and *unlike* his pre-resurrection body. We should expect the same of the resurrected world. It will not be totally different. God declares, "Behold, I am making *all things new*" (Rev 21:5). God doesn't say, "I am making *all new things*." He's not scrapping everything and starting over. Rather, he's purifying the present creation. The story of the Bible begins with a physical creation and ends with a new physical creation.

Throughout Rev 21 and 22, this new creation is described in different ways: as a new world, a new city, and a new garden. And we're told that many things will be missing. There will be no mass chaos, confusion, or terror. Natural disasters: gone. Mobs and violent protestors: gone. Terrorist attacks: gone. Events like 9/11: gone. There will be no personal pain: "He will wipe away every tear from their eyes, and death shall be no more, neither shall there be mourning, nor crying, nor pain anymore, for the former things have passed away" (Rev 21:4). Do you feel the personal touch of God? God himself will wipe away every tear from your eyes. Do you feel the permanence of the healing? Pain, mourning, and death: gone. Forever gone. In the new creation, death itself will die.

In addition to these blessed absences, there is a glorious presence. In the new creation, we will experience the *immediate* presence of God. Currently, God is present throughout his creation, but his presence is hidden from us; it's a *paradoxical presence*: we sense his closeness, and we interpret certain events as evidence of his activity, but we don't see him. Not yet. In the new creation, we will experience the presence of God in a new way. The old creation will be emptied of every destroyer and filled with the divine presence—God's radiant presence: "The city has no need of sun or moon to shine on it, for the glory of God gives it light, and its lamp is the Lamb" (Rev 21:23).

Moreover, we learn that the gates of the new city will never be shut (Rev 21:25). No locked doors, no borders, no foreigners, no exclusion—only embrace. In the beginning of the biblical story, Abraham and his descendants are chosen by God, blessed to be a blessing to all nations. God called Israel into existence for the sake of the nations of the world. In the new creation, people from every nation are present, because the Lamb was slain for "every tribe and language and people and nation" (Rev 5:9). People from every nation are present, because the church has fulfilled her calling to bear witness throughout the world.

Finally, in Rev 22:1–3, the new creation is portrayed as a new garden:

> Then the angel showed me the river of the water of life, bright as crystal, flowing from the throne of God and of the Lamb through the middle of the street of the city; also, on either side of the river, the tree of life with its twelve kinds of fruit, yielding its fruit each month. The leaves of the tree were for the healing of the nations. No longer will there be anything accursed, but the throne of God and of the Lamb will be in it, and his servants will worship him.

These images, and especially the tree of life, should cause us to recall Eden, the first garden of God, described at the outset of the biblical story. God's final redemption of the earth will reverse the curse of Genesis—"No longer will there be anything accursed" (Rev 22:3)—repairing all that was broken in the beginning:

Our relationship with God.

Our relationship with others.

Our relationship with creation itself.

This connection between Eden and the new creation is crucial if we are to understand *what* we will be doing for all eternity. Just as we need to drop the unbiblical idea of floating up to heaven as our final destiny, so we need to drop the idea of harp plucking as our ultimate purpose in the afterlife. While it's right to speak of worship as the activity of eternity, worship must be defined not simply as playing instruments and singing but as living purely for the glory of God, using fully all the gifts that God has given us.

In the first garden, God commanded Adam and Eve to create and cultivate. Remember the cultural mandate? In the final garden, our work of culture making will continue. But it will no longer be frustrated; it will take place within the context of a restored relationship with God, with others, and with creation. All that Adam and Eve were designed to do in the beginning but failed to accomplish because of their rebellion will be fulfilled in the new creation. Here's what this means, in very practical terms. I love writing. It's one of the creative capacities God has given me. But in this world, writing can be very difficult, for a variety of reasons. Publishing deadlines. Rude people who distract me. Migraine headaches. In the new creation, I'll be able to do what I love to the glory of my Creator without any of these things that make writing so difficult.

What do you love to do? What creative capacities has God gifted to you? The resurrection of the body in the new physical creation means the resurrection of your creative capacities so that you can glorify your Creator for all eternity. Imagine building things without the limitations of a budget. Creating art without the fearful thought "What if nobody likes this?" Playing your favorite sport without the worry of injury. Some have suggested that in the new creation there will be better Beethoven. Better poetry. Better drama. New advances in technology. New adventures in space travel. We will glorify God in ways that surpass our wildest dreams.

If ever there was a happy ending to a story, surely it is this one:

God's universal people.

In God's final place.

Living under God's immediate rule.

Fulfilling our God-given purpose.

Forever.

Discerning Deep Stories and Dwelling in the Great Story

"You best start believing in ghost stories, Miss Turner. You're in one."

—*CAPTAIN HECTOR BARBOSSA*

EVERYONE DWELLS IN A STORY. To dwell in a story is to *live* in it. To find in it a home for the heart. To bring to it life's most profound questions:

Who am I? The question of identity.

Where do I fit? The question of belonging.

What difference do I make? The question of purpose.

Everyone dwells in a story. Some story. Facing this reality is the first step toward making a deliberate decision to dwell in a specific story. The Great Story. The Story of Scripture.

Let me show you what I mean. It'll take us a few minutes to get there. But hang with me. It's important. *Really* important.

Our world is a storytelling world. All around us are cultural texts, and together these texts tell the deep stories of our day. In the opening essay of the book *Everyday Theology: How to Read Cultural Texts and Interpret Trends*, Kevin Vanhoozer (brilliant scholar, wicked beard) encourages us to develop "cultural literacy." What is "cultural literacy"? Let's start with the word "culture." Culture is what we make of what God made. Culture is what we get when humans work with the raw materials of nature to produce something. To speak of culture is to speak of the products of everyday life: films and books; cars and clothing; our homes, classrooms, and offices, and all the devices and instruments that fill them. The products of culture are everywhere. And what is most familiar to us often is the most difficult thing to see.

Vanhoozer helps us see what is right in front of us by changing up the vocabulary. Rather than cultural *products*, he insists on the term "cultural *texts*." Your iPhone is not a cultural product; it's a cultural text. Texts convey messages. Texts must be read, interpreted, evaluated. They require critical engagement, not passive consumption. And it's not just your iPhone that requires critical engagement; it's your Instagram account, the ad on YouTube, the characters in the show you binge-watch, and the checkout aisle at your preferred grocery store. As we read the various cultural texts of our day, we'll begin to discern the deep stories these texts convey, meta-narratives that seek to capture our hearts, that seek to guide us to "the good life."

Here's an example. One of the early essays in *Everyday Theology* is entitled "The Gospel according to Safeway: The Checkout Line and the Good life." As Jeremy Lawson, Michael Sleasman, and Charles Anderson interpret the checkout line at their preferred grocery store, observing the print media and assortment of other items carefully arranged in that gauntlet gallery through which we all must pass (unless you Instacart), they discern the following deep story. These are the seven pieces to the good life, according to Safeway:

1. Intimacy: And more specifically, a hyperactive, experimental, open sex life. You can't possibly be happy if you're living a celibate life. Or if you're tied down to one person for life.

2. Beauty: How do you get that incredible sex life? Well, you must be physically beautiful, of course.

3. Health: Related to this, you must have a particular type of physique. Certain proportions. Certain sizes. And a magic number on the scale marks the limit of health and beauty: "Beauty weighs less than _____."

4. Information: You can't have the good life without being in the know. You need information. Information on your sports team and South Sudan. On local elections and the global economy.

5. Convenience: And you simply must be able to attain this information—and whatever else you might need—quickly and easily. *Fast* food. *On-demand* viewing. *Real-time* reporting.

6. Wealth: You can have all these things if you have wealth. Money buys pleasure and power. The problem-free life is available, if only you have the cash—or the credit limit.

7. Celebrity: Sexually fulfilled, physically stunning, instantly informed, and mega-wealthy, you'll achieve the most coveted status of our day: you'll be a celebrity.

The takeaway: *There is no neutral, non-storytelling space.* Everywhere we go, everywhere our children go, cultural texts seek to cultivate us. The checkout line seeks to capture our hearts. Our devices seek to disciple us. The deep stories all around us seek to draw us into their depictions of the good life.

If this is what we're up against, how, then, do we dwell in the Great Story? The Story of Scripture. The only story that reveals our true identity, place, and purpose. *We must develop rhythms that possess the power to re-story us.* That's crucial, so read it one more time. *We must develop rhythms that possess the power to re-story us.* We counter story with story, and we fight rhythms with rhythms. I visit my local grocery store at least weekly. That's a rhythm. Weekly, Publix attempts to draw me into its depiction of the good life. Daily, my social media feed does the same. What I need, then, are daily and weekly rhythms that will re-story me, practices that will anchor my heart afresh in the biblical story. Briefly, here are three such practices.

First, develop the rhythm of personal Bible study. Knowledge of the whole biblical story will give deeper meaning to the individual parts. Recall the quote from *Avengers: Endgame* with which this book began: "I love you 3000." Having seen the whole movie, I hear more in each part. In these four little words, "I love you 3000," I hear an epic battle between the forces of darkness and light and the victory that comes through the strength of sacrifice. This simple line reminds me of the grand story; the part draws me into the whole. Mindful of the meta-narrative of Scripture, we will now begin to hear more in each part. Genesis, Job, John, and James all will draw us anew into the great drama of redemption, the story that runs from creation to new creation.

Second, develop the rhythm of community. Stories are re-called, retold, and relived in community. The Great Story is best heard, studied, and practiced in the context of a small fellowship of believers, an intimate companionship of travelers. The Southern writer and peacock lover Flannery O'Connor said in "Writing Short Stories" that a story is good when you continue to see more and more in it. The biblical story is an inexhaustible well, a bottomless mine. Always, there is more to see. Our brothers and sisters in Christ will find gems in the mine that for whatever reason escape our eyes. To use the language of Jas 1:22, together we'll be better *hearers* and better *doers* of the word; we'll participate more faithfully in the drama of redemption. What the rising number of churchless Christians fail to understand is that solitary spirituality is a shortchanged way of life. In almost all cases, studying the story of Scripture in community will deliver greater treasures, deeper transformation. Though sometimes, it'll trigger a tangent on ghost aliens.

Finally, develop the rhythm of worship. Historic Christian worship has a narrative arc that rehearses the drama of redemption. In his book *You Are What You Love: The Spiritual Power of Habit*, philosopher James K. A. Smith explains that historic Christian worship draws the congregation into a story with four chapters: gathering, listening, communing, and sending. The God who created us in his image, redeemed us in his Son, and empowers us with his Spirit initiates the worship time; he gathers us as his people. Having been called into the presence of the holy and forgiving God, we then enter into the listening chapter of worship. With reverence and eagerness, we attend to the preaching of the word, another opportunity for us to see ourselves as characters in the Great Story. The worship time culminates in our communing with God and with our brothers and sisters in Christ. Communion, or the Lord's Supper, isn't just a way to remember the good news of the Great Story; it's a feast that nourishes us as characters within this story. Having been invited into God's presence, having received the divine will in his word and spiritual nourishment at his table, finally, we are sent into his world to fulfill his mission: to make disciples, be a blessing to all nations, and fill the earth with image bearers. To put it plainly, worship *is* a weekly re-storying.

Everyone dwells in a story. Some story. The deep stories all around us seek to draw us into their depictions of the good life. And more often than we care to admit, they succeed. This is why both you and I need the rhythms of personal study, community, and worship. These are simple things, yes, but they do something profound *to us*. They restore us. They restore us by re-storying us. They anchor our hearts afresh in the story of Scripture. The Great Story.

Bibliography

Allers, Roger, and Rob Minkoff, dirs. *The Lion King*. 1 hr., 28 min. Walt Disney Pictures, 1994.

Augustine. *Confessions*. Translated by Henry Chadwick. Oxford: Oxford University Press, 1991.

Bartholomew, Craig G., and Michael W. Goheen. *The Drama of Scripture: Finding Our Place in the Biblical Story*. 2nd ed. Grand Rapids: Baker Academic, 2014.

Beale, G. K., and Mitchell Kim. *God Dwells Among Us: Expanding Eden to the Ends of the Earth*. Downers Grove, IL: InterVarsity, 2014.

Clements, Ron, and John Musker, dirs. *Moana*. 1 hr., 47 min. Walt Disney Pictures, 2016.

Columbus, Chris, dir. *Harry Potter and the Sorcerer's Stone*. 2 hr., 32 min. Warner Bros., 2001.

Cosmatos, George P., dir. *Tombstone*. 2 hr., 10 min. Buena Vista Pictures, 1993.

Cosper, Mike. "Demon Hunting." *The Rise and Fall of Mars Hill* (podcast), September 10, 2021. https://www.christianitytoday.com/ct/podcasts/rise-and-fall-of-mars-hill/mars-hill-podcast-mark-driscoll-demon-hunting.html.

Cuaron, Alfonso, dir. *Harry Potter and the Prisoner of Azkaban*. 2 hr., 22 min. Warner Bros., 2002.

Dever, Mark. *The Message of the New Testament: Promises Kept*. Wheaton: Crossway, 2005.

———. *The Message of the Old Testament: Promises Made*. Wheaton: Crossway, 2006.

Edwards, Gareth, dir. *Godzilla*. 2 hr., 3 min. Warner Bros., 2014.

Favreau, Jon, dir. *Cowboys & Aliens*. 1 hr., 58 min. Universal Pictures, 2011.

Goldsworthy, Graeme. *According to Plan: The Unfolding Revelation of God in the Bible*. Eugene, OR: Wipf & Stock, 2000.

———. *The Goldsworthy Trilogy*. Milton Keynes, UK: Paternoster, 2006.

Green, Michael. *Evangelism in the Early Church*. Rev. ed. Grand Rapids: Eerdmans, 2003.

Hooper, Finley, and Matthew Schwartz. *Roman Letters: History from a Personal Point of View*. Detroit, MI: Wayne State University Press, 1991.

Hunter, Trent, and Stephen Wellum. *Christ from Beginning to End: How the Full Story of Scripture Reveals the Full Glory of Christ.* Grand Rapids: Zondervan, 2018.

Hurtado, Larry W. *Destroyer of the Gods: Early Christian Distinctiveness in the Roman World.* Waco: Baylor University Press, 2016.

Jackson, Peter, dir. *The Lord of the Rings: The Two Towers.* 2 hr., 59 min. New Line Cinema, 2002.

Lawson, Jeremy D., et al. "The Gospel According to Safeway: The Checkout Line and the Good Life." In *Everyday Theology: How to Read Cultural Texts and Interpret Trends,* edited by Kevin J. Vanhoozer et al., 63–79. Grand Rapids: Baker Academic, 2007.

Lucas, George, dir. *Star Wars: Episode IV—A New Hope.* 2 hr., 1 min. 20th Century Studios, 1977.

Mendes, Sam, dir. *Spectre.* 2 hr., 28 min. Sony Pictures Entertainment, 2015.

Nolan, Christopher, dir. *The Dark Knight.* 2 hr., 32 min. Warner Bros., 2008.

O'Connor, Flannery. "Writing Short Stories." In *Mystery and Manners: Occasional Prose,* edited by Sally Fitzgerald and Robert Fitzgerald, 87–106. New York: Farrar, Straus & Giroux, 1957.

Ross, Gary, dir. *The Hunger Games.* 2 hr., 22 min. Lionsgate Films, 2012.

Rowling, J. K. *Harry Potter and the Sorcerer's Stone.* New York: Scholastic, 1998.

Russo, Anthony, and Joe Russo, dirs. *Avengers: Endgame.* 3 hr., 1 min. Walt Disney Pictures, 2019.

———. *Avengers: Infinity War.* 2 hr., 29 min. Walt Disney Pictures, 2018.

———. *Captain America: The Winter Soldier.* 2 hr., 16 min. Walt Disney Pictures, 2014.

Smith, James K. A. *You Are What You Love: The Spiritual Power of Habit.* Grand Rapids: Brazos, 2016.

Spielberg, Steven, dir. *Raiders of the Lost Ark.* 1 hr., 55 min. Paramount Pictures, 1981.

Taunton, Larry Alex. *The Faith of Christopher Hitchens: The Restless Soul of the World's Most Notorious Atheist.* Nashville: Thomas Nelson, 2017.

Tolstoy, Leo. "How Much Land Does a Man Need?" In *How Much Land Does a Man Need? And Other Stories,* translated by Ronald Wilks, 96–110. London: Penguin, 1993.

Toro, Guillermo del, dir. *Pacific Rim.* 2 hr., 12 min. Warner Bros., 2013.

Vanhoozer, Kevin J., et al., eds. *Everyday Theology: How to Read Cultural Texts and Interpret Trends.* Grand Rapids: Baker Academic, 2007.

Verbinski, Gore, dir. *Pirates of the Caribbean: The Curse of the Black Pearl.* 2 hr., 23 min. Walt Disney Pictures, 2003.

Waititi, Taika, dir. *Thor: Ragnarok.* 2 hr., 10 min. Walt Disney Pictures, 2017.

Waldron, Michael. *Loki.* Disney+, 2021.

Whedon, Joss, dir. *Avengers: Age of Ultron.* 2 hr., 21 min. Walt Disney Pictures, 2015.

Young, Terence, dir. *Dr. No.* 1 hr., 49 min. United Artists, 1962.

Made in the USA
Monee, IL
25 August 2022